Big Dog and Little Dog
Wearing Sweaters

Dav Pilkey

Houghton Mifflin Harcourt
Boston New York

www.hmhco.com

Library of Congress Cataloging-in-Publication Data is on file.
ISBN: 978-0-544-53097-3 paper-over-board
ISBN: 978-0-544-56237-0 paperback

Printed in the U.S.A.
MER

45007752555

Ages	Grades	Guided Reading Level	Reading Recovery Level	Lexile® Level
4–6	K	D	5–6	240L

To Robert Martin Staenberg

Little Dog has a sweater.

Big Dog does not have a sweater.

Big Dog is sad.

Big Dog wants a sweater, too.

Big Dog is looking for a sweater.

Little Dog is helping.

Big Dog has found a sweater.

Hooray for Big Dog!

Big Dog is putting the sweater on.

Little Dog is helping some more.

Now Little Dog has a sweater.

And Big Dog has a sweater.

Big Dog and Little Dog
are warm and happy.

Good night.

 Lost in the Maze

Can you help Little Dog find a sweater for Big Dog? Use your finger to trace the path!

❧ Word Search ❧

Find the hidden words from the story!
Remember, words may go across, down, or diagonally!

Word Box

SWEATER	DOG
HELP	HOORAY
WARM	HAPPY
BIG	LITTLE

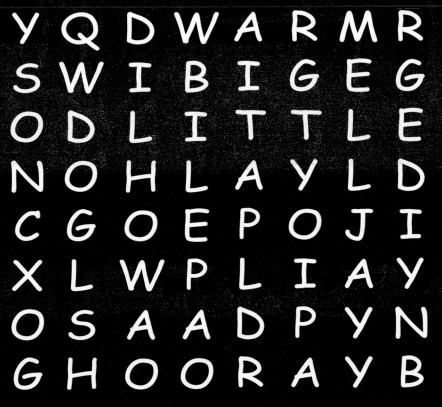

```
Y Q D W A R M M R
S W I B I G E G
O D L I T T L E
N O H L A Y L D
C G O E P O J I
X L W P L I A Y
O S A A D P Y N
G H O O R A Y B
```

✿ Story Sequencing ✿

The story of Big Dog's sweater got scrambled!
Can you put the scenes in the right order?

A

B

C

D

E

🐾 Picture it 🐾

Read the sentences below.
Point to the picture that matches each sentence.

Big Dog does not have a sweater.

Big Dog has found a sweater.

Little Dog helps Big Dog put on the sweater.

Big Dog and Little Dog are warm and happy.